AGAINST SUNSET

AGAINST SUNSET

POEMS

STANLEY PLUMLY

W. W. NORTON & COMPANY

Independent Publishers Since 1923

New York | London

For information about permission to reproduce selections from this book,
write to Permissions, W. W. Norton & Company, Inc.,
500 Fifth Avenue, New York, NY 10110

For information about special discounts for bulk purchases, please contact
W. W. Norton Special Sales at specialsales@wwnorton.com or 800-233-4830

Manufacturing by RR Donnelley
Book design by Chris Welch
Production manager: Lauren Abbate

Library of Congress Cataloging-in-Publication Data

Names: Plumly, Stanley, author.
Title: Against sunset : poems / Stanley Plumly.
Description: First Edition. | New York : W.W. Norton & Company, [2017]
Identifiers: LCCN 2016022703 | ISBN 9780393253948 (hardcover)
Classification: LCC PS3566.L78 A6 2017 | DDC 811/.54—dc23 LC record available at
https://lccn.loc.gov/2016022703

W. W. Norton & Company, Inc.
500 Fifth Avenue, New York, N.Y. 10110
www.wwnorton.com

W. W. Norton & Company Ltd.
15 Carlisle Street, London W1D 3BS

1 2 3 4 5 6 7 8 9 0

For Margaret

Day unto day uttereth speech,
night unto night sheweth knowledge.

CONTENTS

I

II

III

ACKNOWLEDGMENTS

Thanks are due the editors of the following magazines in which poems in this volume—many with revision—originally appeared: *The American Poetry Review, The Atlantic, Harvard Review, The Georgia Review, The Kenyon Review, Mare Nostrum, The New England Review, The New Yorker, Ploughshares, Poetry, Poetry Northwest, Smartish Pace,* and *American Writers Respond to September 11, 2001,* edited by William Heyen (Etruscan Press, 2002).

My endless gratitude to my friend David Baker and my editor Jill Bialosky, whose continued support makes all the difference. Gratitude as well to Rob McQuilkin.

And my deepest appreciation to Lindsay Bernal, Michael Collier, Howard Norman, Jane Shore, Joshua Weiner, and David Wyatt, colleagues and eternal friends.

And grateful thanks to the Graduate School and the University of Maryland for its ongoing support.

AGAINST SUNSET

I

DUTCH ELM

I miss the elms, their "crowns of airy dreams,"
as Virgil calls them, their towering cathedral branching
spread into a ceiling above the lonely sidewalks of Ohio
where the first elm deaths were reported in America.
I miss in particular the perspective looking down
the distances of all those Elm-named streets disappearing
into dusk, the last sun turned the stained blue of church windows.
I miss standing there, letting the welcome dark make me invisible.
I miss the birds starting to sleep, their talking in their songs becoming
silent, then their silence. I even miss not standing there.
And I miss a life of nothing but such moments, as if they'd never
happened and all you had to go on was their memory
and the feeling in the memory forgotten but brought back
again and again because you miss someone you loved forever.

BROWNFIELDS

The early eighties
and we're living south of Hampstead,
on Grantully Road, next to Maida Vale, in spring,
a raw, rare season of Constable-size clouds
coming in off the Atlantic on their way to the Channel,
the darker the heavier the rain.

We have a place three floors up
with a view of Paddington Recreation Ground,
which, now the snow is gone, is under
the plow entirely. Renewal or revival, who can tell?
From the windows, after storms, what we see,
surrounded by the city, is a park

turned into empty and emptier country,
acres of scabby mud thawing in weak sunlight,
then in the longer rains, something
like a potter's field awash in potsherds.
So one Sunday, ankle-deep, we go wading,
picking among the scatter

of what has been a landfill
for eighteenth- and nineteenth-century
cracked or flawed Wedgwood—serving bowls and cups,
tureens and dinner plates with scenes
of rural life, bric-a-brac perhaps,
and lavish urn-like shapes

meant for death or human waste,
    festooned with flowers and bunch-of-grapes
and the full and tender leaves of Arcadia,
    now broken down to broken bones
and carried in house buckets to a bath
      in order to be picked among again,

    like the piece I have in hand.
    Years later, I'm standing at the grave
of Keats, wondering what to steal, token Keatsiana,
    when the god of the discarded
builds for me a mountain, a mound of Roman potsherds
      named Monte Testaccio,

    here within the meadows of lovers
    and dead poets, Cimitero Acattolico,
just inside the city of the old Aurelian Wall—
    Shelley, Shelley's son, Severn and Trelawny,
and the four thousand others among the weeds
      and grasses, cypresses and pines.

    Like every other griever,
    I choose a flower, a violet, "Resurrecturis,"
in stone, above the iron main gate.
    In St. Matthew 27, the Sanhedrin seek out counsel
for blood money no one wants
      now that Judas has repented,

which is the sum, exactly,
　　to buy the potter's field to bury strangers,
outsiders, the meek and very poor,
　　as if to put back into lesser earth
those of lesser parts. When I was small,
　　　　closer to the ground,

　　　I'd see things no one else could see,
　　which may be why my father made me
follow him down foundry garden rows
　　of digging, pulling, picking,
waste not, want not, though what I'd find
　　　　among potato vines

　　　and corn was coins
　　and Shawnee arrowheads and ingots into stones
and flints and rusted cartridges—
　　and coral-colored shells shattered
into seeds, as if a sea, upon a time,
　　　　had planted them.

WITH DEBORAH IN AMHERST

Out of the blue, out of the marble blue
of her eyes, the sudden tears—we'd be talking
about dinner, where to go, already driving,
the forsythia burning sunlight into evening,

passing—of all possible places—
Emily Dickinson's house and what was once
The Evergreens, where Austin and Sue Dickinson
wore a daily path back and forth.

It'd been a hard cold year, snow on snow
piled up roof-high, with all the windows covered—
who doesn't blame the weather when the weather
takes over, transference or too much exposition.

If fear is a cover word, pain is a better word,
a blood word, that cuts like paper or a clean razor.
It wasn't tears exactly, or only, but her body
breaking open the whole hurt length of it,

as if, in that moment, she'd halved her heart,
the mind, in that moment, now a body all its own.
She'd have put her head in her hands and leaned over,
sobbing into the dead space under the windshield,

so I'd have stopped the car and we'd have
started walking back and forth, on Main,
in front of the wrought-iron fence—
or was it white and wood, painted every year?—

that serves as a separation between worlds,
the Dickinson museum and the present tense.
"The Things that never can come back, are several—"
there were other times we'd be sitting in the driveway

and her face would fill with grief, change all the light
around her, and she'd almost start to scream,
then think about it, then scream a single syllable,
then swallow it, and like machinery, shut it down.

Where does it begin—long-suffering sorrow?
It builds a house and over years begins to tear
at it, brick by eaten brick, as ice eats
the ground, and the ground turns back into a field.

"Childhood—some forms of Hope—the Dead—"
such a mixture of failure and failed love,
a time-line as a lifetime, as if our lives were linear,
ours or anyone's. I remember, most of all, the trees,

their classic stature, their first-growth size, and how,
in late September, they seemed to die with color:
that outsized oak that took up all the lawn
in the front of where we lived on Blue Hills Road,

beautiful, like weather or wild nature, and again,
always to be blamed. The trees, everywhere around,
loomed like other century presences. Who knew, in such
an old, deep place, how quickly trees humiliate our losses.

DREAM

There's a scene in which we're standing in a room,
talking, almost touching, and she's looking almost
past me through the window, into the never future:
she's telling me to leave or—the way things happen
in a dream—to simply disappear, her hands lifted
flat against the air, as if to stop a train or break a fall:
suddenly I see I'm nothing in her eyes except the light
flying in her direction from places in the past so far
from here they'll be already gone by the time the light
arrives: this on a schedule—if it's real—like a memory,
though more like a feeling too distantly remembered,
the way a thing that happened takes on a separate life
and in the middle distance of the night wakes you and
for that moment your mind is adjusting to who knows.

LOVE POEM

Someone in the driveway taking your name in vain.
Someone in the dark in the driveway taking your name in vain.
Someone in the middle of the night in the driveway
taking your name in vain. Someone whose voice carries.
Someone standing on the flat black surface of the driveway
whose voice reaches floor above floor with the clarity
of causes, standing very still with her hands at her side,
speaking in an octave between the moment and memory,
ascension and descent, the way singing climbs a ladder
then, step by step, backs down, only to lift itself again.
Someone in the driveway looking up at the windows
with a voice like eyes. Someone with the words, standing
in the darkest well of dark until first light and the birds
and the leaves this way and that way in the wind.

VARIATION ON A LINE FROM ELIZABETH BISHOP'S "FIVE FLIGHTS UP"

Sometimes it's the shoes, the tying and untying,
the bending of the heart to put them on,
take them off, the rush of blood
between the head and feet, my face,
sometimes, if I could see it, astonished.
Other times the stairs, three, four stages
at the most, "flights" we call them,
in honor of the wings we'll never have,
the fifth floor the one that kills the breath,
where the bird in the building flies to first.
Love, too, a leveler, a dying all its own,
the parts left behind not to be replaced,
a loss ongoing, and every day increased,
like rising in the night, at anytime a.m.,
to watch the snow or the dead leaf fall,
the rings around the streetlight in the rain,
and then the rain, the red fist in the heart
opening and closing almost without me.
"—Yesterday brought to today so lightly!"
The morning, more and more, like evening.
When I bend to tie my shoes and the blood
fills the cup, it's as if I see into the hidden earth,
see the sunburned path on which I pass
in shoes that look like sandals
and arrive at a house where my feet
are washed and wiped with my mother's hair
and anointed with the autumn oils of wildflowers.

TERMINAL INSOMNIA

Maybe it's the night-shift-like long hours,
maybe it's the dark, or nothing more
than mirror water in the street,
the habit of the soul to think,
or the wave, its undertow, continually
arriving, what my mother called the ocean,
the shell inside the ear. Then there's
the granular, neutral substance of the air,
its small gray forms of privacy . . .

And a story in your head about new life
and death, about the birth umbilicus
wrapped around your neck, rotting at the navel,
your face already blue, the rest of you
in blood and needing blood, the needle
in your nothing arm to save you,
the memory now a scar of your mortality,
like the fact of being born,
all of it made real by separation.

At least if you're awake you're alive,
though the rain's almost alone enough
to make you close your eyes,
the rain that's summarily, only dying.
The night, entirely on its own, is dying,
as the circulatory systems of traffic
and the birds and the white sun
on the city take their time taking over.
Lie down, lie down with me at dawn,

and float among the rushes on the edges
of the Nile, the White and the Blue,
the longest river on the earth,
where night will pass right through you,
so that in the morning Pharaoh's daughter
will discover you and wake you
and lift you into the dream world with tears,
"Because I drew him out of the water,"
and because of the tears.

JACK GILBERT

The one time I met him was at Halpern's
30th Street & Fifth Avenue apartment,
nineteen seventy-something, on a roof
that doubled as a sort of garden space
where, on other occasions, Dan would roast
a pig and we'd drink to the open sky
or the cumulonimbus clouds drifting
full-blown on parade—Gilbert came right
at me, white wine tight in hand, almost
nose to nose, "I'll bet it's Stevens,
not Williams," a bet he would have won,
having read me pretty well, with an Old
Testament judgment that I was wrong
and doomed. He wasn't tall, though he
had a face sharpened with an edge of mind
that seemed to cut the air, like the quartz
cut to flint inside his poems. Later,
I remembered his picture on the cover
of Gerald Stern's *Red Coal*, the two of them,
as young men, walking toward the camera,
talking with their hands, completely
unaware they'd live a whole day longer,
with Paris at their backs, or that old
age would mean they'd both survived,
like Jeffers, Pittsburgh, as Stevens,
at the end, survived Hartford, Williams,
East Rutherford. If poetry is one silence

speaking to another silence or otherwise
communities of spirits, Gilbert's is
somewhere in between. He lived on islands
of his own making. White islands
in waters crystalline. His obit quotes
a friend that Gilbert was our "greatest
living poet," a large and loving claim,
which we all are, ditto, until we're dead.

CRASHING AT BILL'S AFTER MY CLASS AT NYU, TWO BOTTLES OF ITALIAN RED, REAL STILTON AND SOME BRIE AND ALMOST STALE SALTINES

I'd have already started with the students at the Knickerbocker,
the taxi taking no time to 123rd and Amsterdam,
Bill watching the late game on the Coast,
then another hour of drinking as we'd toast the gods
of loss, eat, and divide, as with a knife, the poets from the rest.
Perhaps it would be raining, snowing or a mix, the slick streets
sending up too much noise and cold, sometimes
the sound of a garbage truck, sometimes only a siren.
At one point he'd begin to read translations of his Martial
or the new poem that day to fill the day. At one point,
maybe this one, we'd reached the hour of wisdom.
Who will love us in the end? That came up a question.
By three, by bedtime, by long after, we'd have had to pee again:
I was in the end room of the Pullman train apartment,
sometimes in the hall we'd sort of have to pass,
Bill's poignant white-bread body moving like a ghost,
my own pale weaving being a figment of my lit imagination.
He was, now that I think about it, dead.
I was dead too but didn't quite yet know it.
The train had long since left on schedule headed west—
first under the Hudson, then the Garden State,
then memory, open country, Pennsylvania, then Ohio.

MORTAL ACTS

The way to reach you at your one-room
Village fourth-floor walk-up was to call
from a booth across the street, after which
you'd show up at a window, if only
to make sure, then work your way down
the narrow half-lit stairs to unlock the door—
a single bed, a table and a straight-backed
chair, a lightbulb and a Frigidaire,
and a payphone on an aging yellow wall.
You hadn't been there long, the job
at Binghamton meant traveling by bus
or driving to the center of the state
where the noir-in-color painter Edward
Hopper had once made lonely art of
Depression downtown buildings bleaker
than the rail yards and B&O freight cars.
In the end you couldn't do it, drive or take
the bus, be that tired again, so you won
the Pulitzer and efficiency apartment
that goes with full professorships at nearby
NYU, as close as you could get to home
in faraway Vermont. The penny-on-the-tracks
you gave me I still have somewhere
in a drawer, where, over time, it's taken
on a small life of its own—I'm thinking
of that afternoon in Athens, in Ohio,
when your old insomnia and chance

of sitting down permitted you to fall asleep
reading *Body Rags*, your forehead
on the desk; and thinking of our gathering
that church-filled Sunday reading Smart
when we were all amazed at how you saved
Rukeyser from sinking from the script
by lifting, by her elbows, her concentration
back to the lectern and the words,
as if no one were the wiser, least of all
the reader; and of that night in bitter cold
Ann Arbor, with an audience of hundreds,
when I asked if you would read the elegy
for Derry, and you said no then yes
then depended on the pages you surely
knew by heart, that are so difficult
to get through to their certain open
end where they struggle to assert how
the dust swirled into a man has but
one shape that is that man, even as his
death heals what he suffered, and how
those who loved him know this until they die.

TO AUTUMN

A walk along the water meadows by the playing fields
of the college—a mile-and-a-half to the hospice
of St. Cross—a walk he takes almost every day
in "the pleasantest town I was ever in,"
including a Sunday named for the sun cutting angles
with its scythe, when it strikes him just how beautiful
the season has become here at the end of summer,
the gathering of light, the harvest coming in,
"chaste weather—Dian skies . . . a temperate sharpness."
He writes Reynolds that he "never liked stubble fields
so much as now . . . Somehow a stubble plain looks warm—
in the same way that some pictures look warm—
this struck me so much in my Sunday's walk
that I composed upon it." Then he forgets to enclose
what it is he's composed, so writes immediately
to Woodhouse about how cool the evenings are,
and that "I should like a bit of fire to night—
one likes a bit of fire—How glorious the Blacksmiths'
shops look now—I stood to night before one till I was
      verry near
listing for one. Yes I should like a bit of fire—
at a distance about 4 feet 'not quite hob nob'—
as wordsworth says . . . You like Poetry better—
so you shall have some I was going to give Reynolds—"

What distracts us makes us. "To night I am all in a mist;
I scarcely know what's what"—this is what he gives
to Reynolds. "It strikes me to night that I have led
a very odd sort of life for the two or three last years—
Here & there—No anchor." Like his bankrupt brother
George, in the middle of America, he's penniless,
in debt, and in fear of the Winchester jail.
"In my walk to day I stoop'd under
 a rail way that lay across my path, and ask'd myself
'Why I did not get over' Because, answered I,
'no one wanted to force you under'—
I would give a guinea to be a reasonable man—
good sound sense—a says what he thinks,
and does what he says man—and did not take snuff—
They say men near death however mad
they may have been, come to their senses—
I hope I shall here in this letter—
there is a decent space to be very sensible in . . .
I have been at different times so happy as to not know
what weather it was—No I will not copy a parcel of verses.
I always somehow associate Chatterton with autumn.
He is the purest writer in the English Language.
He has no French idiom, or particles like Chaucer."

BEAUTY

The dead snow piled head-high at the corners,
whatever winter light there is broken where
the ground has lifted up the sidewalk, black ice
on the street like the surfaced backs of whales—
took a ride on the cleared roads in the country,
snowfields filled with crows among the geese
feeding on the cornstalk stubble from the summer,
and higher up a hill a blanketed bay mare warm
against her foal, a few black cattle, too, drifting
with the piles of barn-dried hay, and a few inland
gulls whiter than the snow against the sun,
then acres of untouched covered pasture,
air on the windshield made clearer pushed—

II

RED BRICK

What is the brick thinking, Louis Kahn asks,
holding it up in front of the class
in his forgotten son's film about him,
what is the will of the brick.
What is the will of the brick?
I'm thinking, in the brick by brick of mind,
of all those broken sidewalks, studded streets,
those long walks looking down,
counting, lost in thought,
and, looking up, those bricked-up Methodist churches
of childhood, and the lifting, to my father,
of red bricks from a ladder,
the small serrated edges, textures, shades,
and slightly various sizes
with the branded names of kilns,
my mother's patient longing for the beauty of a house
the wolf inside the wind cannot blow down,
the weight of brick, the war of brick, the ruin of brick,
the trapped air within and in between
its pocked and porous nature,
the mason with his stellate trowel,
his chalk- and mortar-whitened hands,
the level of the depths he's built,
the plumb line of the verticals,
the scaffolding, the worn-out planks,
the hod that's sometimes spilled—
and then those times, like now, remembering

the looming, aging brickwork of a wall
at the far end of a London street
I lived on all those years,
its planetary presence absolutely out of Dickens,
its darkness and its rightness monolithic . . .
in the morning rags of rain,
by afternoon the sun rekindling the fire
it first came from, the whole high reach of it
high enough the English sky won't fall
nor the English ground give up its gravity,
as more than once I pressed my palm against its heart
to feel it breathe, to feel it move, to let it go
and walk away in order to give it distance.

MY NOIR

In nineteen forty-nine we still have inkwells with ink bottles
in carved-on hardwood desks that are bolted to the floor,
with cast-iron scroll grillwork for legs, the whole assembly
wholly elegant in an antique way. Somebody loves
somebody whose capital initials are dug in wide and deep,
and more than one obscenity is sanded out but clear,
plus spilled ink stains that some days look like maps—
I've written on and written at these desks, learned to draw
each letter like a drawing, and learned to spell my name
wrong with an *e*—not Stanley but Plumly—learned
the hidden art of paying no attention in favor of the windows
in the spring that open on the fat oaks just outside
and are locked against the winter and catch-your-death-
of-cold—how deep the snow printed on a page . . .

It's a test, of some childishness, to hold an open hand up
to your face, in the pitch dark, to see if you can see it—
most of the time it's never dark enough, so you have
to close your eyes, though at Piqua's Little Theater,
when the western film would break, there'd be those
inkblot moments nothing could be seen, except the exit sign,
your still eyes still adjusting from the action on the screen,
your impulse to complain with catcalls overwhelming.
At what age is the night world first made real to us?
I mean made real in front of us and at the same time
at a distance, as if you're here and somewhere else at once,
the way, holding up my hand as if to blind to my face,
I could feel my breath breathing back at me, until
the cone of smoke blue light shone again with cowboys.

I think I was fifty, *Night and the City* on a special
double bill, end of the day, slipping into dark,
London imagined "at the violet hour" bruised over bright
in a film-slick after-rain, the hero-fool running for his life
against the credits: London imagined as an aftermath
to war and its survival, a noir-lit world regardless of the hour,
the ceiling sky a darkness all its own: Widmark, Tierney,
characters as fate, as fate as character is arbitrary,
the plot almost always just the same: you die, I don't.
Which is it, in the end, we love the most, the thing itself
or the picture of the thing? The daylight at noon
or the matinee? Or dark to dark, our made-up movie lives?
The killers are absurdities with stage names or their own,
Herbert Lom, Mike Mazurki, Stanislaus Zbyszko—

at a certain age on certain days you identify with everyone.
When I was told to write within the half-inch of the lines
it seemed a lot of trouble, so I'd send an arrow here or there
or let the rainbow at the curved top of an *O* rise above
the absolute horizon—a question, constantly, between success
and failure—though this was nothing to the nothing
on the paper when nothing was exactly what it was,
an emptiness demanding to be filled, and there you are,
yourself and no one else, staring at a space with nothing in it.
What if your whole life is colorless yet flammable as camphor
(and nitrocellulose), a celluloid where countless lives
are written passing through, three or four or more of whom
may matter, though there are hundreds who fade away
in sunlight, and a few who almost lasted but finally disappeared?

I remember, my first year there, you still needed coupons
for sugar, flour, and salt; or am I too in sympathy with war,
since supply and demand simply made things more expensive—
one thing, for sure, traveling on the buses or passing on the street,
"the silences were palpable" and made you feel outside,
as at a window looking in: London as beautiful as ruins,
and at night, among the ghosts, an "unreal city" of the dead,
but beautiful and vast, 1666, 400 acres, 10,000 houses,
St. Paul's and 80 churches, a holy fire to purge it of its sins . . .
O burn it down and build it up again for floating bombs
and rockets to purge its innocence. I'd start my walks at dusk,
from Green Park to the Heath, four miles or more, depending,
the color of the clear sky failing blue before the Irish clouds
and Irish rain could kill the evening air drifting off the Thames.

Keats, a mid-May morning, out on his Hampstead lawn,
writing against a deadline he imagines to be real, writing
the night bird singing into life the long death of the day,
on stanza scraps of paper whose order is obscure—writing
against the hours of the sun still rising, the early flowers growing
at his feet, his brother Tom now buried where "Beauty cannot keep
her lustrous eyes," while here "but to think is to be full of sorrow."
I'd sometimes walk past midnight, then read, the light tossed
on the pavement through the window, outside from inside . . .
Keats was my book, I could see him with a lantern on the same
street path from town, too poor to pay the coachman, too proud—
"Keats" a name made up and written on good paper that is still
only paper, then word for word a story like a fiction of a fact
no one alive remembers, the reader all alone, a shadow in the room.

The movie dark, the way it loves us, keeps us to itself.
Richard Widmark is unworthy of Gene Tierney, who will have
to watch him strangled and dropped into the Thames, broken
by the men who were chasing him at the beginning of the picture.
I know this scene is something more than what it is, in keeping
with Keats's observation that every life of worth is a "continual
allegory," even a life that's worthless as a warning sign or symbol.
The Curzon was doing a Tierney festival—*Leave Her to Heaven*
the other picture, in which she's a killer, too, watching a cripple
drown. I couldn't believe it, wouldn't believe it, didn't believe it,
yet Widmark dies believing Beauty has betrayed him and is watching.
No one, not even on the screen, can run fast enough, far enough,
or find a dark that's dark enough to hide in—when the mixed mind
went there it was crowded, like a shelter, with strangers.

Sweet river of Edmund Spenser, dark river of Charles Dickens.
Were you to stand in the middle of one of the many bridges
in the middle of the night, looking down at the soft fires moving
on the surface, letting the soft air rise and cool your face,
the dark itself like the depth of the river, thick enough to fall
safely through: were you to stand there, looking down,
as free of thought as it is possible to be, able at last to see,
the way, when you were a child, you would cover your eyes
in order to feel the true warmth of the dark, the night voice:
were you to stand there, out of time, meaning outside of time,
you would have to decide whether or not, though the decision
had been made, since to imagine it is to do it, to dream it awake—
London, up and down, the serpent of the Thames impossible
to follow and more impossible to know, from here, to its end.

September 3, 1802, "Earth has not anything to show more fair"
than London at dawn from Westminster Bridge, as the city
"now doth, like a garment, wear/The beauty of the morning . . .
Ne'er saw I, never felt, a calm so deep!"—the sun rising
out of sleep, Wordsworth, in his century, another witness.
Better to be still for as long as you can stand it, stand still
as if outside yourself, in the second, then the third person,
the spiritual or the long perspective: is it when I left my body
or when my body left me that I understood why night is the open heart?
All the parks of Greater London dote on chestnut trees, fantastic
in their symmetry, too vulnerable to time, their bell-shaped flowers
in spring like candelabra, their yellow autumn horseshoe-shaped
bright leaves brighter in the dark, so that in the summer dusk,
between these extremes, you loved it under the branches looking up.

THE SLEEPING DOGS OF ERICE

At half-a-mile the thirty marble churches and cobbled
marble streets feel light as air above the sky-blue depths
  of the Tyrrhenian, feel able, in fact, to float as on the platform
of the mountain of a cloud, La Montagna del Signore,

  though the plural would make more common sense
since the gods of the many mountains around the Mediterranean
  have each had their day conquering the history of the island,
arriving in a morning fog from sea on a schedule fit for war.

  Right now, first light, the night ghosts of the air have risen
off the sea or fallen from the sky or both at once, it doesn't matter—
  from this balcony it's as if we have ascended into life
in a wholly different way, purer in the purity of *il velo di Venere.*

  It will take all morning for the mist to disappear,
especially from the slick stones of medieval village paths
  that still pass for streets and the shining stained-glass windows
so bright they'll stop the sunlight until the afternoon:

  which is when I see them first, curled up for naps
in an awkward weedy courtyard, four stories down, spaced
  as if assigned. Six of them at least, though their numbers tend
to change, depending on the day and where they trail,

usually at the edges of the town: which is when I see them running,
sometimes chasing, sometimes playing, but always together,
    but not always, because the large dog lying or sleeping in the traffic
of the Piazza Umberto, is, I'm sure, at heart, one of them—

    lean the way these hunters are living off the land:
the kind, when I was a kid in the country of Ohio, we called strays,
    dogs who'd been let out from the backs of trucks or cars to die
or survive, burned with sores and starving. These, though, are Italians,

    Sicilians, who understand the value of community and numbers,
the civilizing forces of the pack, so that when I see them now
    at different times at different intermissions, nuzzling or mating,
I'd swear they are eternal: of the mythic body back to the nursing

    loving founding of Old Rome, mist turned into stone,
and stone turned, inevitably, to ruin, back into mist, as they too
    are quarried, cut to shape, interchangeable through time,
and for a while the drained-blood lilac color of white marble.

TRAVEL IN THE AFTERLIFE

You go there and you're no one anyone has ever heard of,
which is exactly what you hoped for, including the erasure
of your passport, your old body what humanity, generally,
comes to look like. As for the language, in a boulangerie-
patisserie near Saint-Sulpice you were hungry for a sandwich
but suddenly struck dumb, so gestured to your mouth
and managed a croissant—almost what you wanted—
the busy Paris French, still perfect in their clothes, looking
now away from a dead American pointing with his finger
at his face. Not that different from the time in the Piazza
del Popolo when you closed your tourist eyes in the middle
of a crowd in order to imagine another, different life
from the one that brought you here, and kept them tightly
shut so you could see inside the stone cobbled on the street
and lifted into buildings ancient in the air: and see the sunlight
in the stone, the shining centuries of rain, the ending beauty
of the moment's certain future, with a fountain in the square,
large autumnal trees, a pretty wind, and tables, and Romans,
no, Parisians passing in their pairs, as if alive, back and forth.

And if you count the sanderling exactly the number
I saw on the beach at Duck, seven at the water, feeding,
twelve in a line along where the tide had ended, watching.
One of those accidents of timing that greets the very nature
of artifice, the way William Debrae, my great-grandfather,
taught me the art of the kite at the edge of the ocean at
Kitty Hawk or at the edge of a lake that looked to me
like a sea, who had, for truth, bought his schoolteacher
bicycle from the Wrights in Dayton at the beginning
of the twentieth century, and who was born before our
Civil War and knew survivors of the War for Independence.
Nothing is disconnected, the numbers plotted, cause-and-effect,
persons, places, things that seem so arbitrary until you think
about the man at the dead end of the pier waving his arms.

SEASONAL

Late Winter Dusk

Out of my mouth a thrush, a spotted leaf,
invisible among all evening things,
the sun having passed almost completely
through the piping of the new snow in the trees.
When my thrush sings it speaks, I think, in clear
"liquid ethereal tones" to hold off
the night-long vacancy of dark. What is it
about this dying time of day we love,
no one else, in the moment, alive,
the streetlights still not on, then starting on,
the last hour colder than the one before,
the bone-bark plane trees higher than the roofs,
filled to the top with bells, this hermit thrush
or wood thrush having arrived too early?

Beach Reading

The angles angling down on the ocean's broken surface,
while overhead the spirit of a remnant vapor trail.
Then half-looking into the sun's dead reckoning,
enough that behind the fire in each eye blood,
but only for the blinding rainbow moment.
Then back to blue, back to the stone-shell colors.
Then the loose scarring—or is it scarves?—
of thinning cirrus clouds floating on the light's
transparency just above what looks like wings or sails
stroking the horizon. Then in the middle distance
dolphins double plowing to make furrows
and off and on the diving birds and skimmers.
Then the moony children and the mothers, and simple bodies
wading out to sea, the brightness turning barely into breakers.

"I Have Been at Different Times So Happy

as to not know what weather it was."—Keats.
But I'm thinking, nevertheless, how fine this day is,
what the poet, in a different moment, calls
"chaste weather—Dian skies," meaning the slightly
speckled robin's-egg blue autumn air is holding its color
longer than it has to in sunlight almost thoughtful,
its clarity the kind of honesty you want to join
so completely the heart disappears or, exactly the other way,
is enlarged: a feeling second only to the changes
in the leaves, their mid-season off-reds and -yellows,
their sheer love of the wind, their surrender in parts;
and to the sudden shapes of birds moving into,
moving out of the trees, night starlings mixed with
house "citizen" sparrows, countless until you count them—
these, in this moment, and the leaves, and the fine dry air
to see through, seeing as into a feeling without meaning.

December

Hard to tell
what looks like the stillness
of a bird from the outline of a leaf
among the scatter of what's left
on the plane tree bearing down
on the window, here on the page,
there, just outside, though I know
what I see as I know the air in the room
is a wall and beyond the wall
the far dark is an abstraction,
like a tree at night,
rain in a rill inside the branching,
the wind sometimes lost in the sorrow spaces—
and right now it could be dawn, cold dawn,
or the end of the day,
first light or last light holding on,
shining in a something-year-old tree,
where a bird, at the bird-height of trees,
could be a dry leaf curled,
the sun having started
or run through its spectrum,
depending on the colors, added or subtracted,
a healing, a wounding, morning or evening,
though you know, without saying, which one.

Minutes ago, roof-high above the driveway,
a red-tail, with three, four angry crows—gone
and gone, the still air gray and heavy after rain.
The book is beautiful, its artful glossy pictures
a perfect elevation of watercolors, oils, and a few
pencil drawings, whether or not the birds are exactly
that exotic or simply richly painted, the three kinds
of predatory hawks wild-eyed and gorgeously rapacious,
the Northern Eagle Owl like royalty enthroned,
the Golden Oriole all gold, even the Jay's blue headdress
almost burning off its head. Art is the transformation of the real,
though what the degree the change is something else.
Picasso, who rarely painted birds, claims all art is abstract.
Like words, and words' wasted breath, especially written down.

It is hard to tell if my hawk was chasing or being chased—
I could see the dried blood color of its tail. Life
is kinetic; art, like the art of birds, a form of stasis,
as static as Eliot's Chinese jar moving perpetually
in its stillness. Audubon shot his birds as cleanly as possible,
so that, posed, they became another thing, a third thing between
life and death. He seemed to need the model in the flesh.
I doubt the other artists here have his shooting skills.
They must have worked from memory or photography,
in an order of a picture of a picture of a picture,
given that what imagination is, is built from image.
My favorite is Paul Barruel's *European Robin*, a softer warmer
version of the American living bird, as if he'd used pastels
instead of watercolors with the downplaying effect of a dry brush.

SHELLEY'S ARROGANCE

I've seen storms like his/one time, on a balcony,
looking out into the darkest part of the morning
above Lake Lecco it woke me, the lightning arcing
the water between the tops of the lake's green hills
below the ghostly snow-capped Alps/
though at the Tate you can see the fiery English version
of great storms alive in the Turners by just standing
there/"For God's sake reef your sails or you are lost"/
"I am borne darkly, fearfully, afar"/I think I know
what Shelley means by fate, which is to say what looks
like life invented in a painting or a story or a poem
is actually a life planned right up to the end after which
we say how perfect/his poem for Keats may well be
a highly well-wrought "piece of art" thought out
in a boat ahead of a thunderstorm the year before
he sails from Leghorn/but it is, as Mary says, an elegy
for Shelley/foreshadowing that long day of "dead
calm—the atmosphere . . . oppressive . . . the sun excessive"
until it all suddenly changes into a sky of "smoke and rags"/
Adonais lifts him, he claims, above "the stormy mist
of sensations"/yet there he is "one white and tranquil
sail to leeward against a turmoil of black cloud"/
"I die like mist upon the gale"/so little of him left
from falling through the sea into the mouth inside the sea/
ten days and Keats's book of poems to help say who he is
in pieces washed ashore/what seems to be the heart
the shape and color of the liver/Byron, a shadow

in a carriage, at a distance, watching the funeral fire/
Trelawny lifting from the ash the fragment of a jawbone
he saves as a souvenir/Hunt imagining the blue Italian
sky bluer by the hour/three hours of burning driftwood.

PAUL GUEST ADDRESSES HIS APPLE WITH A STYLUS

The reason, at this moment, I'm thinking of Richard Nixon
is Louis McCallay, nineteen sixty, when we argued about Kennedy
and this man you would never buy a used car from
because of his stuttering eyes, the anger in his mouth,
the school-paste pallor of the skin pulled loosely over his face,
and, most of all, the Ed Sullivan shoulders. Louis was a Scot,
with the kind of native thrift that when you wash your hair
you wash it only once, and he was going to donate Nixon money.
I washed his hair, just once, almost daily, as I washed him whole
each day, his ancillary penis no less flaccid than his flesh,
the way, too, his bowels had always to be helped,
his urine self-sufficient through a tube.
And when he wasn't flat as paper in his bed,
he dressed like an Ohio Republican, Yale tie, J. Press,
wing-tipped oxford shoes, then, chair by chair, I carried him.

He died in increments, disappearances, wealth . . .
I hope, regardless, that some part of him has passed through
the eye of the needle, especially because, right now,
I'm listening to a young man on a stage—who's twice
the paraplegic Louis was—reading from a screen his purity of poems
controlled by a sort of stylus tucked carefully yet lightly
into the corner of his mouth, who's so lost in a long deep thought
that were he alone he would write it.
Louis loved the thought of moving through time-lines,
from Paris in the thirties to London in the sixties
or else in the abstract vision of a book, say something like
the four embodiments of Swift's Lemuel Gulliver,
who, in sequence, is too small, too large, not smart enough
to be the high mind over matter, but who finally comes to know
the separation of the soul from a different kind of body.

And who, returning home from all his various voyages,
can no longer stand the sight and smell of family,
so must go out to the stables to be again with horses,
the result of a condition T. S. Eliot defines as a "dissociation
of sensibility," who himself identified with the fourth world
of the *Travels*, not unlike the world in which we've all tried to leave
the tragic version of ourselves far enough behind to forget it
or accept it as words and nothing more.
But because we live in language, Swift chooses "houyhnhnm," for human—
no, perfection, in beings wholly other, in bodies wholly beautiful.
Paul Guest is reading to an audience his poems.
The room is enormous, the sky-domed ceiling vaulted,
the silence like another voice filling the empty space.
And I'm listening and thinking of the distances
imagination travels sitting still, wandering in all directions.

MANHATTAN

A man on the sidewalk, lying down,
eyes straight up, smiling, an astronomer,
taking in what he can of Jupiter and Venus,
in their together moment in the cut-out of the sky
above the Park at 88th—
one of those blue-black clear June nights, nothing
but the atmosphere between the earth and no one,
the crowd from the Guggenheim thinking
he's just street art, giving him as wide a berth as possible.
The vertical picture, true north, "the dizzy heights,"
we used to call them, turning in a circle in the summer in a field.
Stand at noon at the base of any one of the city's twentieth-
or twenty-first-century skyscrapers and try to sight your way
all the way to the top and you'll probably fall over—
a kind of vertigo reversed—
since a high-poetry-of-mind wants to take you,
in Wallace Stevens' "Supreme Fiction" phrase,
to "the celestial ennui of apartments,"
which you can almost see with a hand over an eye,
though this would never work for the tucked-in summit
of the Empire State or a building like the aspiring
needle-pointing Art Deco Chrysler Building,
as it folds to a slightly scalloped pyramidal crown,
unless you're looking from the glassed-in-eye-level of a high-rise,
Third Avenue or Lexington or somewhere stationed in the air.
Fly in, however, late at night, before 9/11, especially in love,
the pilot standing on a landing path along the whole East Side,
all the buildings' left-on lights stellar
over the river and the FDR . . .

ASPECTS OF THE NOVEL

One thing after another—a sequence or a consequence,
narrative or plot, on Friday the once-upon-a-time wife dies,
on Sunday the once-upon-a-time husband dies of grief
or a death to that effect, cause because she dies as an act of will.
Someone's always left behind, married to the old address,
in medias res, as in the middle of a field, where it may
or not be possible to read between the lines
before the dawn burns off the layers of the mist
those mornings like the afterlife of night.
She dies as an act of will, which is a story.
I'm thinking of the life of a man looking back who asks
was any of it real, now that he's locked inside his history.
If there are pictures, what are they worth—?
When we turn toward the camera's shutter speed,
in that moment of the theft of soul, are we still alive?
I look at her in black-and-white, hear her voice, try to remember,
though the story's now so far in the storied past
I wonder if it matters. Was it real, or is it written down?
In the falling dream when we fly we fly all the way to ground
or otherwise wake up, holding on.

EARLY NINETEENTH-CENTURY ENGLISH POETRY WALKS

1

I remember the rain, a cold coin-colored all-day rain,

hard as coins, straight down, June, just outside of Keswick,
walking like a tourist in a light raincoat, soaked through,
imitating Wordsworth heading north from Grasmere to meet
Coleridge heading south, probably in the same rain but in Macks,
the bed-and-breakfast no less damp, and breakfast—how many
hours ago—a wet porridge and a kipper. And how many shades
of green, each of them electric, how many shades of limestone,
sandstone, shale, alliterative as hillocks and small mountains:
Keats and Brown in this same rain, too, "a sort of grey black mist . . .
Our road a winding lane, wooded on each side . . . full of Foxgloves."
Death weather, as far as I can tell, the visible breath like fog,
the chill air "fledged with Ash & other beautiful trees," five miles,
ten miles, Helvellyn then Skiddaw in an outline of themselves.

2

The need for names—to shape and map the glib amorphous earth,
including the one circumambient ocean: here, in pools of lakes
and falling, snow-fed rivers, scarp and scar and cove, the lesser
elevations labeled tors, the deep depressions, vales: Derwentwater,
Duddon, Blind Tarn, and Old Windebrowe, Lorton and Long Meg,
the grammar school in Hawkshead where Wordsworth carved
his name indelibly in oak in letters more a sign than signature . . .
At Dove Cottage, still a hundred and sixty-some years on,
you could hold an original Wordsworth in your hands,
both manuscript and book, and walk away, the living word
even more alive on dead rewritten paper. "Wordsworth's name
is nothing—to a large number of persons mine stinks," so writes
Coleridge in his Coleridgean logic to keep their names unsigned.

3

Wordsworth past his prime, Coleridge, a ruin, sequestered
in Highgate for his health: Keats writes his brother George,
in the wilds of America, that on this 28th of June, 1818, Keswick,
"I have slept and walked eight miles to Breakfast—we could not
mount Helvellyn for the mist so gave up with hopes of Skiddaw . . .
The approach to derwent water is rich and magnificent
beyond any means of conception—the Mountains all round
sublime and graceful and rich in colour—Woods and wooded
islands here and there"; then, abruptly, breaks this tour guide to say
"We will before many Years are over have written many folio volumes
which is a Matter of self-defence to one whom you understand
intends to be immortal in the best points and let all his Sins
and peccadillos die away," and it isn't clear if he means poems or . . .

4

Keats has met and already judged Wordsworth—now, mid-April,
1819, "Last Sunday I took a Walk towards highgate and in the lane
that winds by the side of Lord Mansfield's park I met Mr Green
our Demonstrator at Guy's in conversation with Coleridge—
I joined them, after enquiring by a look whether it would be agreeable—
I walked with him at his alderman-after dinner pace for near two miles
I suppose." Keats adds, based on this singular encounter with
the one and only Coleridge, that "In those two Miles he broached
a thousand things—let me see if I can give you a list—Nightingales,
     Poetry—
on Poetical sensation—Metaphysics—Different genera and species
of Dreams—Nightmare—a dream accompanied with a sense of touch—
single and double touch—A dream related—First and second
consciousness—the difference explained between will and Volition—

5

so many metaphysicians from a want of smoking the second
consciousness—Monsters—the Kraken—Mermaids—southey believes
in them—southeys belief too much diluted—A Ghost story—
Good Morning—I heard his voice as he came towards me—I heard it
as he moved away—I had heard it all the interval—if it may be called so."
Coleridge's account is that their meeting lasted "only a minute or two,"
and that Keats was either "a loose, slack not well-dressed youth"
or "a young man of very striking countenance"; and that, parting,
"when I shook him by the hand there was death!" In both their hands.
Perhaps, at the beginning, every poet thinks, like Keats, that
"I am however young writing at random—straining at particles
of light in the midst of a great darkness," and we'd have meant it,
late into the night, kept up, like Coleridge, listening to nightingales.

6

That moment when the three of them decide to walk to Scotland,
in August, from Grasmere—Dorothy's idea, hoping to repair the rift
between her brother and the now rheumatic Coleridge, except
it's the North and there's insufficient laudanum to sustain
their brilliant friend, so by the time they cross the Borders,
it's already two hard weeks against addiction. Friendship is what we have
and fail. Coleridge turns around, walks home, wherever home is.
Bone-chilling cold like ice inside the rain, two hundred and sixty-three
long miles in eight long days, including an arrest at Fort Augustus
and no shoes because he's burned right through them trying to dry them.
Five years before, Sara has nearly burned through those same shoes,
or shoes just like them, as if to anoint his feet with boiling milk,
though this time there'll be no walking, only writing, as Coleridge

7

takes Wordsworth, Lamb, and Dorothy on an imaginary tour
in his mind of his favorite after-dinner evening stroll that turns out
to be a "Homewards" journey. "Der Wanderer," the " Journeyman"—
two ways biographers elevate the addict's need to move, move on,
Highgate, at the last, his home. Wordsworth chooses Rydal Mount
as the place to live and die, the place he's not at home when John
Keats comes to visit, who leaves a thoughtful note and discovers
on the mantel his modest book of poems with the pages still uncut,
the ill beginning of a walk of revelation and destruction: first the Dumfries
tomb of Burns—"not very much to my taste"—then an enervating side trip
to Ireland, green with poverty, then back to Burns's poor birthplace in Ayr—
"dirty bacon dirtier eggs and direst Potatoes with a slice of Salmon"—
in keeping with a body of a thousand mortal days, almost to the month.

8

Burns's "disposition was southern—how sad it is when a luxurious
Imagination is obliged in self defence to deaden its delicacy
in vulgarity, and riot in things attainable that it may not have
leisure to go mad after things which are not." Or on the other hand,
writes Keats, "One of the pleasantest means of annulling self is approaching
such a shrine as the cottage of Burns—we need not think of his misery,"
though Keats does, and writes page on page to his dying brother Tom
that "We can see how horribly clear in the works of such a man
his whole life . . . he talked with Bitches—he drank with Blackguards":
who sees himself in Burns, and after a month of Mull, Fingal's Cave,
and climbing to the raw tiptop of Nevis, he is done, sailing back to London
on a smack, "too thin and fevered to proceed." Wordsworth had written,
when Keats was only seven, that "We Poets in our youth begin in gladness;/

9

But thereof comes in the end despondency and madness," and Burns
is the plough poet he has in mind. And he adds, in the same walking
poem, an even stranger warning, that "By our own spirits are we deified,"
as if the poet has the power, in nothing but the words, to rise from the paper,
the way Thomas Chatterton, "the marvelous Boy," invented language.
What is experience except its words?—Wordsworth climbing Snowden
in a mist, the night closing in, the moon "naked in the heavens . . . /
A hundred hills their dusky backs upheaved . . . /In headlands, tongues,
and promontory shapes . . . /Thus might we wear a midnight hour away."
Darkness on a mountain, the spirit of the place invisible in light.
No different in the Alps, at Simplon's Pass: "I was lost as in a cloud . . .
Imagination! lifting up itself /Before the eye and progress of my song/
Like an unfathered vapour—here that Power . . . /came athwart me."

10

"Our destiny, our being's heart and home,/Is with infinitude,
and only there," what Wordsworth also calls "the invisible world."
But what if what's invisible is real because it's visible, like a mountain
or a lake, or, if you're Charles Lamb, and lonely out in nature, the city
and its crowds a kind of countering?—"Give me a walk in the bright
piazzas of Covent Garden." Then he asks of the deep Wordsworth,
"Have I not enough without your mountains? I do not envy you.
I should pity you, did I not know, that the Mind will make friends
of anything. Your sun and moon and skies and hills and lakes
affect me no more than . . . a gilded room with tapestry and tapers,
where I might live with handsome visible objects. I consider the clouds
above me but as a roof beautifully painted"—perhaps by Constable.
"Old chairs, old tables, Streets and Squares . . . these are my mistresses."

11

Walks. Coleridge walks, at his best, through abstraction thick as glass,
toward what Hart Crane calls "an improved infancy," both his son's
and his own. There is no stopping Coleridge. Shelley, "borne darkly,
fearfully, afar," tries to walk on water, "far from the shore." Keats,
in the thousand days before the end, walks in ever-closing circles.
"I was a Traveller then upon the moor . . . as happy as a Boy,"
writes Wordsworth, still poet in his youth, though on that path
he sees "a Man before me unawares:/The oldest Man he seemed
that ever wore grey hairs": both of these are Wordsworth,
going and coming back: "the whole Body of the man did seem/
like one whom I had met with in a dream;/Or like a Man from some
far region sent," who'd started out a fell destroyer, thief
of a shepherd's boat, a skater at the wheeling center of the lake.

12

Keats walking into town to see himself eighteen hundred years ago—
"I cannot bear the City though I have already ventured as far as the west
end for the purpose of seeing Mr Haydon's Picture," in which Lamb
is the namesake innocent, Wordsworth is a monk, and Keats himself,
in profile, is on fire, but right now in a corner of the famed Egyptian Hall
he's trying to disappear. Christ is entering Jerusalem on a donkey, Palm
Sunday, the crowd in the painting swarming all around him, a hundred
fifty square feet of new faces, each of them immortal, as long as paint lasts.
In eight months Keats will be walking north on the west coast of Italy,
yet not exactly walking but at a walking speed in a small Roman carriage,
surrounded by the wildflowers Milton builds in "Lycidas" or like the flowers
in "Nightingale"—violets and the musk-rose and "pastoral eglantine"—
or flowers we've never seen by other names, funereal and beautiful.

13

The rain is falling, falling from afar. Nothing in nature would not be
better off without us. Wordsworth walking is looking for something,
first in the moment, then in "Those recollected hours that have the charm/
Of visionary things," in which poetry "is fashioned and built up/
Even as a strain of music." Coleridge is walking at a thinking pace,
though no less in prison than in his lime-tree bower, the image of an idea
that "Nature ne'er deserts the wise and pure" perfect in his heart.
"Mountains, Rivers Lakes, dells, glens, Rocks, and Clouds . . . Grand,
    sublime"—
Keats is in Rome climbing the Spanish Steps in order to promenade
the Pincian Hill. It's winter so the dark falls faster, faster than the rain.
"Tell him," writes his London friend Leigh Hunt, in a letter he'll not
receive, that "he is only before us on the road, as he was in
everything else, and that we are coming after him." And have.

III

TOO BROAD A BRUSH THE *FIELD GUIDE TO THE NATURAL WORLD OF WASHINGTON, D.C.*

By Howard Youth, especially its section on its birds,
when it's one living bird, buoyant on a cattail
at the edge of a Maryland pond, trilling its mathematics
into song, that really matters, then full silence, then again,
in keeping with disguise, the way this blackbird is blacker
with the wet sheen of a crow, formed to the size of a cardinal.
It's when it flies in front of you from one place to another,
across the bike lane to the pond's other side, that you see
the show of the shoulder, the scarlet cut on the wing
above the cut of the yellow, like an epaulet for honor.

It's as difficult to translate birdsong as it is to translate poetry.
Does the red-wing "belt out a rusty-hinge-like Konk-la-Ree!"
or is it more of a zreeeee zrr zrr or "a simple raspy z-z-z-
z-z-z-z, almost insect-like"? I hear it and what I hear
is antediluvian, back to when the marsh was the meaning
of dry land—what I hear is primal, territorial, without apology.
What I read in the field guide is that the territory "vigilance
of male red-wings may protect yellow warblers that nest
nearby from marauding . . . cowbirds." Song for song.
The first red-wing I ever really heard I saw sitting
on a fencepost in Iowa, resting in the cut corn of the sun,

after the summer harvest. It can take a long time in a lifetime
to hear, to see a thing. I was in my thirties, in the fly-over heart
of the country, and some days so lost I'd drive the county roads
just to watch the wind shear inside the great machines—row
after row, the blackbirds gathering, like gulls, in the combine's
sudden wake. I must have needed to be there in order to see
the beauty of the bright wounds on their wings in the late
September light. And as they flew they sang, though it's
in the field guide that males will sometimes ride the backs
of herons and red-tailed tolerant hawks as part of
their attacks on intruders, singing something like a rattle.

SUICIDE

Something to think about, an abstraction,
like being, therefore I am, I am whatever.
Like the spirit bird in reaction to nothing
it can see except itself flying over and over
into the icy window. Perhaps the sunlight
in the room reflected in the glass that brings
to life what otherwise looks cold is fire enough.
Break the bright window and everything changes.
Those days we think we want to die and know
this, too, passes are like those images of flight
the imagination loves, as there we are, watching
the winter cardinal so suddenly out of breath,
taking a moment, taking it in, its sunlit wings
unfolding on the branch, ready to try again.

LIMITED SIGHT DISTANCE

That afternoon we'd finished up early, at about two-fifteen, and decided, since it was a particularly pristine day, to make the long descent into town. Maybe to get coffee, shop, whatever. We were fifteen minutes getting ready, and it would take fifteen minutes more to reach the exit gate.

We were in lucky residence at the Villa Serbelloni, centerpiece of the Rockefeller Foundation fifty-acre holdings spread out on the high hillside overlooking the village of Bellagio at the meeting place of Lakes Como and Lecco. The villa and its grounds and gardens are a sight to behold, located among some of the most beautiful mountain borders in the world, the Pre-Alps, as they're called, which serve as grass and granite precursors to the real Alps, the great gray mountains whose ghostly, snowy forms loom almost invisibly.

Much of this height and majesty are grounded in water, in the famous Italian lakes out of which they rise. The lakes are vast, and the rich moraine shore that constitutes the hemline around them is peopled with innumerable lovely towns, Bellagio being the "Pearl of the Lake," as Shelley once wrote. Lake Como is the largest and deepest.

Anyone who's been to Bellagio knows the beauty of the place, its special lakeside, mountain character in the midst of what surrounds it, sitting as it does at the very tip of Punto Spartivento, "the point that divides the wind."

The boat and ferry traffic on the lakes is not only necessary but from a position of perspective gorgeous to watch, while the long drives around the lakes are no less spectacular. The charm of the whole area derives in part from its narrow-road, waterborne separation, even isolation from an otherwise busy Northern Italy.

This was a warm, sweet day—big, clear blue overhead, blue-green in the distant view of the water. "Veduta" means view in Italian, and from top to bottom, from the villa down to the village itself, and from the tops of the cobblestone streets to the diamonds on the lakes, the view is everywhere, from every moment.

Walking the elegant switchback path into town it's all visible all at once—the sky, Lake Como, and the green, sheer mountains in between. You could lose your balance stopping on the descent and looking up or out too long, the way, in Manhattan, when your eye follows the upward line of a skyscraper into the open sky you tip over.

We reached Via Garibaldi, the main one-way circular through-road well before three, well before nine in the morning on America's East Coast. Judith went into the pasticceria for biscotti and to chat with Maria, the owner. I sort of lingered on the street, people-watching and looking up at the great sky, heavenly blue.

A loud TV voice started coming from the coffee bar nearby. The sound had clearly been turned up. It straightened my attention—I hadn't heard an American amplified for quite a while.

I followed the voice, then there it was: a grand glass tower on fire, with equally billowing gray-black clouds worming their way a few floors from its top. On the modest screen it all seemed smaller than it was, like special effects. I remember that, and remember that I wasn't certain where it was happening—Boston, perhaps, the Hancock Building, the voice-over saying something about Logan Airport.

Planes run into mountains, I thought, not buildings. CNN was going back and forth between English and Italian, both of which constituencies, plus a few others, were beginning to crowd the little bar. Then we saw what came to be known as the second plane swoop in and make its turn and crash into a now suddenly apparent, within the window of the screen, second tower.

This was live. The tourists and locals who filled the confinement of the space spoke out in their several languages, bewildered, many in tears. The point that divides the wind, the end of an island.

And here we were, on another kind of island, heaven on earth, someone within my hearing had called it. It tested one's sense of reality, especially since the messenger was television, the ultimate verisimilitude, the medium that needed to print *live*, like a label, in order to distinguish the living from the taped. I was sure there were those in this audience thinking to themselves that the whole thing was a movie.

I went outside to find Judith, who was just emerging from the pastry shop, and pulled her in among the rest of the witnesses. I didn't have to say anything, the scene had become immediately apprehensible. The barman had by now switched the TV exclusively to English. I couldn't watch anymore.

It was four or so, Italian time. And all the shops had reopened from their long lunches. And it was September 11, the day John Keats had had to return, in 1819, to London from Winchester to try to raise money for his brother George in America, who had been swindled into bankruptcy by John James Audubon. Keats would fail his financial mission, though a week later he would write "To Autumn," his last and best lyric poem. I'd been taking notes on this interlude in Keats's short life when we'd taken our break to walk into town.

Of the many terrible images of that terrible day one that must stand out is the confirming sight of that second plane finding the second World Trade Center Tower and the sequence of death that followed. The small screen in the coffee bar, four thousand miles away, did not diminish nor contain the event. It merely provided an eye and supplied dissociation. When we finally, two weeks later, were free to fly out of Milan for a connection at Heathrow, air space, mind space, heart space were still without schedule.

At Heathrow it was pandemonium, a human mixture of those who had, since the day of the attack, been living at the airport, those who had somehow got there in the meantime, and those, like us, who had been at last granted permission to show up. Reservations didn't matter, nor even first-come, since hundreds in every terminal were vying for the same attention.

Security was somewhere between military, makeshift, and arbitrary, which meant, inevitably, the Middle Eastern population was set apart, though to the degree it mattered we were all now refugees—battering and pushing forward, arguing and insisting, finger-crossing and praying: all to find a seat on the next, whenever that was, plane.

I didn't want to spend another day in Europe. It felt wrong. It felt wrong not to be home. We got blessed and got a flight within twenty-four hours. It was officially autumn.

It felt as if a war had started. The path back on British Air would lead us near New York City, so the pilot steered the plane as close as possible—miles but close enough—and again there was only a piece of window to see through, to frame, to magnify, to bring to scale.

I remember, again, some wept. And I remembered pure late winter nights returning to Manhattan from near and distant places and for the fun of it the pilot cruising, within acceptable space, the length of the island, the whole lit beautiful ocean liner of it.

Here, though, in this interminable moment, at this sad distance, there was only diminishment, a naked sun's neutral glare, and at the south end of the island a void, a filled emptiness of still deadly ragged smoke staining and drifting into the open sky.

POLIOMYELITIS

Magical numbers! Roosevelt the most famous infantile paralysis
adult to ever live with it, thrive with it, die with it, at sixty-three,
contracted at thirty-nine, the same integral number as my birth year
and the year, 1939, when the world war that changes everything starts—
the President treading water with his hands and arms, standing
at poolside in Warm Springs, the life in his legs different from any feeling.
Polio the proof that the child in us never disappears but turns against us
just when we think we've outgrown its memory and become who we are
and were meant to be, a whole other human body with a mind like a city,
more beautiful at night, while the still heart is a pastoral, with a piper.
A man said Roosevelt, at the end, looked like the most dead man alive
he'd ever seen: the girl in the iron lung, too, resembling what children
imagine death in the satin of its coffin looks like, her face roughed up
with rouge, her soft brown hair straightened, the rest of her forgotten.

What does it mean, the kingdom is near in each of us, especially the poor in spirit, when that's the poverty we assign the wealthy? There is, of course, no enemy, except in devils, demons, and ourselves, which on faith we can expel with changes to the heart and acts of will, though wide is the gate and broad the way that leadeth unto death, while strait is the gate and narrow the way that leadeth unto life, yet the night my father fell to his knees surrounded by my mother in the house they had just built and built on rock, his heart changed in a different way and his will narrowed to the size of a broken stone. Who is in charge of the decision we must die, and what of the disciple who wants to depart Capernaum for the funeral of his father only to be told, No, follow me, and let the dead bury their dead—word now made of flesh? So how do we heal the leper? And the multitudes, whose welcome is now worn, who have traveled near and far in order to learn the difficult paths of righteousness, what does it mean to be left behind while the twelve who follow sail to the other shore, as if in search of where to lay their heads? What is the power of a hand to still the storm and calm the waters? Whithersoever thou goest. What does it mean to be a fisher of men?

WITHIN THE HOUR

Him sitting on the edge of the bed with my mother's arms around him,
the one clarifying image of my father near the end,
everything in the bedroom—the air, the pre-dawn quality of light,
the awkward furniture, his nakedness—failing.
Dying's necessarily different from death, the way he's sitting there.
You either know or learn this loneliness.
He wants to die, he doesn't want to die: meanwhile, his heart
is filling up his chest, doubling its weight and workload.
By the time I see his X-ray the heart is something else,
something torn away, the trailing veins attached
like pulled-up roots or the thin-most ends of branches.
You understand that when your own time comes,
all this time your father's lived inside you
with his heart.

LOST THEN FOUND PHOTOGRAPH OF
MY PARENTS

The bleached-out background sky is infinite,
as the picture, like all pictures, seems freestanding,
and, like all pictures, will, sooner or later, be an image
of the dead, including the scythe-like curving of a car roof,
plus part of the post between the two car doors right
behind them: it's probably a Chevy thus a comedown from
my father's Ford convertible, the one my mother's driven
into a tree, at a slow, courtship, side-street sort of speed.
This is marriage, this is still the thirties. Whoever's holding
the camera—a Brownie Hawkeye?—has disappeared as well,
on this, I think, a wedding day or a day just after. They're
dressed in coat and tie and something office-formal
to make the bride look older, with a handkerchief emerging
from a pocket at her heart. Neither one of them seems
happy, unhappy, or unsure, simply unaccustomed
to what, in fact, just happened, death-do-them-part,
my father's squared-off shoulders supported on each side
by crutches, an accident of timing, as most things in a life
tend to be, my mother, on his left, with her faithful look
of faith, since pictures never lie, looking straight at us.

AT THE PICTURE WINDOW

First there's the maple,
still filled out in brick-brown reds and rust,
a few leaves, big as hands, falling, drifting,
then, on a different day,
nailed by the rain to the lawn.
When I was alive, when I was a daydream,
I'd sit in the window's three-cornered bay for hours,
for the thought of it, the secret of it,
the glass and separation,
and if for nothing else the view—
how old was I?—
a farm light here and there now coming on,
the twilight turning deeper bluer blue,
then a childish number of the visible stars.
Then, suddenly, first thing in the morning,
the dry and yellow acres of ripe September corn
fluttering like paper
along the shadow angles of the sun.
Then the sun overhead.
And after school the wasted afternoons,
not a live soul or dead soul anywhere,
except the Amish on their way to mystery
in their elegant cab carriages,
the horses' hooves like clockwork on the asphalt,
a worn-out pickup truck or tractor with its load
slowing to a walk behind them.
Part harvest, part emptiness . . .

Across Scott Garbry Road a brake of brush
and two white oaks that by the early frost
would ring with the madding chatter
of every kind of blackbird, black on black
especially when the guns went off
and the birds rose in swarms of smoke and scattered—
they'd be back, some would, the next blue dusk,
then disappear again, dark and darker,
into the pale night sky,
echoing the sounds of what they were.
Which is why my mother loathed the trains,
their hollow distances and silences between,
trains in the winter,
close enough to see and far enough
to hear their long passing heartbreak
carried by the cold,
floating on the ice and depth of snow,
right up to the porch and through our seven rooms.

RADIO

I couldn't go to sleep without it, the music
of those voices in my head, surviving or dying
as best they could among the sound effects
of footsteps in a hall, city traffic in a cab,
women older than my mother talking girls,
The Shadow's Orson Welles, or an imitator actor
pretending to be him, who knows what evil
lurks in the hearts of men—my own child's heart
already damp with sin—the sometimes rain
of static interrupting what a murder means
or awful love or a dummy mouthing anger like
it's comedy, until *the stroke of midnight*'s signing off,
then birdsong at first light to keep me company.

A MOMENT FOR MAURICE SENDAK

I knew who you were—I'd probably read,
standing in an aisle, a good sample of your *Wild
Things*, thinking to buy a copy for a friend's sick child,
but put it off till later, or never, which is the way
aisle-readers read who don't buy the books.

Exposition is the enemy, or at least too noisy,
like tin cans tied to the tail of the experience—
I'd read more about you than read you,
then the other day picked up a copy of your book
about your brother and Eugene, your partner

fifty years, a book that finally is an elegy.
The day you called to thank me for my *Keats*,
to say how it had saved you after surgery
from suicide or worse, I could hear the oral history
of losses in your voice, hear your Polish family

gone forever in the camps, hear your memory
of the kidnapped Lindbergh baby, hear the Brooklyn
boy inside you still angry, and the wild nights, wild
nights with creatures in the kitchen. Who looks
like that, a heady happy monster, with a carnivore's

sly mouth and the bad teeth of your uncles,
and a roly-poly body both kindly and corrupt?
You must have been almost my age when you called,
days home from the hospital, ready to go back
to reading your classic friends—Shakespeare,

Henry James, George Eliot, and Keats, and, darker,
Emily Dickinson—ready to walk your loved dog Herman
Melville, that you turn into a pig in *Bumble-Ardy*.
You claim in a late interview that your sister's
orphaned children mean nothing to you. Nothing.

"I loved not being dead when I was a kid."

ELEGY

There's that age when we can't look at the face
of the dead anymore, a brother or sister, my sister,
since by blood it's your face too—no, that's too easy:
it's the loved face, the vital living face that's missing
behind the mask and the body like a mannequin's.
Worse, it's the bed, the funeral bed, queen-size sheets
of satin and a child-size pretty pillow and awkward
arms crossed over on the chest and the hands turned
to glass and the coffin like fine furniture with flowers.
Death's odor adds a resonance, like powder in the air.
It's a question, ash or dust, all of her, in a moment,
up in smoke or a leaf-like drying out disfigurement.
Someone has leaned down to kiss her, someone else
has placed a piece of paper at her side. I think it's paper.

AGAINST SUNSET

The California sun an hour, maybe half-an-hour still high,
depending on how fast it falls: where does it go except into the sea,
to burn out blue, blue-green, then finally potash into powder,
like the cocoa-colored settled dust that looks whiter on the moon,
a moon that will soon be rising? Does a stone fall faster than a feather?
Toss an apple into the heavy salt-sea air, up and down—faster?
The feather fell from a white sea-bird, I'd almost eaten the apple.
The horizon, halfway disappeared between above and below—
night falls too or does it also rise out of the death-glitter of water?
And if night is the long straight path of the full moon pouring down
on the face of the deep, what makes us wish we could walk there,
like a flat skipped stone? I've seen the sun-path poured at dawn
on the flat other side of the country, but it was different, the yellow
morning red with fire, the new day's burning hours oh so slowly climbing.

REFERENCES

Epigraph—Psalms 19:2.

"Brownfields," "With Deborah in Amherst"—Deborah Digges 1950–2009.

"Jack Gilbert"—Jack Gilbert 1925–2012.

"Crashing at Bill's . . ."—William Matthews 1942–1997.

"Mortal Acts"—Galway Kinnell 1927–2014.

"To Autumn"—Letters to John Hamilton Reynolds and Richard Woodhouse, September 21–22, 1819, John Keats 1795–1821.

"My Noir"—*Night and the City*, Jules Dassin, director, 1950.

"The Sleeping Dogs of Erice"—Erice, Sicily.

"Nineteen Species of Sandpipers—Sibley"—*The Sibley Guide to Birds*, David Allen Sibley (Knopf, 2000).

"Thanking Friends for *The Art of Ornithology*"—Howard Norman and Jane Shore (*Birds: The Art of Ornithology*, Jonathan Elphick [Rizzoli, 2015]).

"Shelley's Arrogance"—Percy Bysshe Shelley 1792–1822.

"Aspects of the Novel"—*Aspects of the Novel*, E. M. Forster 1879–1970 (originally delivered as The Clark Lectures, Cambridge).

"Early Nineteenth-Century English Poetry Walks"—Letters to Tom and George Keats, June 27–August 6, 1818, and to George and Georgiana Keats, February 14–May 3, 1819, John Keats; letter to Joseph Cottle, Samuel

Taylor Coleridge, May 28, 1798; *Table Talk*, July 21, 1832, S. T. Coleridge; "Resolution and Independence," William Wordsworth; *The Prelude*, Book XIII (1850), W. Wordsworth; letter to W. Wordsworth, Charles Lamb, January 15, 1801; *The Prelude*, Book I (1850), W. Wordsworth; letter to Fanny Keats, John Keats, April 1, 1820; letter to Joseph Severn, Leigh Hunt, February 1821.

"Limited Sight Distance"—a common road sign for hilly, limited sight terrain.

"A Moment for Maurice Sendak"—Maurice Sendak 1928–2012 (*My Brother's Book*, HarperCollins, 2013).